RYAN HOWARD

Power Hitter

By Elijah Jude Gose

 **Gareth Stevens** Publishing

Please visit our Web site www.garethstevens.com. For a free color catalog of all our high-quality books, call toll free 1-800-542-2595 or fax 1-877-542-2596.

Library of Congress Cataloging-in-Publication Data

Gose, Elijah Jude.
  Ryan Howard : power hitter / Elijah Jude Gose.
      p. cm.
  Includes index.
  ISBN 978-1-4339-3653-1 (pbk.)
  ISBN 978-1-4339-3654-8 (6-pack)
  ISBN 978-1-4339-3652-4 (library binding)
  1. Howard, Ryan, 1979- 2. Baseball players—United States—Biography. I. Title.
  GV865.H67G67 2010
  796.357092—dc22
  [B]

                              2009037642

Published in 2010 by Gareth Stevens Publishing
111 East 14th Street, Suite 349
New York, NY 10003

Copyright © 2010 Gareth Stevens Publishing

Designer: Daniel Hosek
Editor: Greg Roza

Photo credits: Cover (Ryan Howard), title page © John Capella/Getty Images; cover (background) © Whit Preston/Stone/Getty Images; pp. 5, 19 © Elsa/Getty Images; p. 7 © Ezra Shaw/Getty Images; p. 9 © Nick Laham/Getty Images; p. 11 Jim McIsaac/Getty Imagesp. 13 © Rich Pilling/Major League Baseball/Getty Images; p. 15 © Rob Leiter/Major League Baseball/Getty Images; p. 17 © Tom Briglia/WireImage/Getty Images; p. 21 © Jamie Squire/Getty Images; p. 23 © Doug Pensinger/Getty Images; p. 25 © Stephen Wilkes/Getty Images; p. 27 © Ronald C. Modra/Getty Images; p. 29 © Jed Jacobsohn/Getty Images.

Printed in the United States of America

CPSIA compliance information: Batch #CW10GS: For further information contact Gareth Stevens, New York, New York at 1-800-542-2595.

Contents

Meet Ryan

Ryan Howard is a pro baseball player.

He plays for the Philadelphia Phillies.

Ryan was born in 1979. He grew up in St. Louis, Missouri.

Ryan played baseball for his high school team. He worked very hard to be a good hitter.

Ryan played college baseball for the Missouri State Bears.

The Phillies

Ryan began playing first base for the Philadelphia Phillies in 2004. He only played in nineteen games.

13

Ryan's first full year playing for the Phillies was 2005. He hit twenty-two home runs that year!

15

Award Winner

Ryan showed everyone that he is a very good hitter. He won the Rookie of the Year award in 2005.

In 2006, Ryan won an award for being one of the best hitters in pro baseball.

Ryan won a Most Valuable Player award

in 2006. He also won first prize in a

home run contest!

World Series Winners!

Ryan helped the Phillies win the World Series in 2008!

Hitting Home Runs

Ryan reached 100 career home runs in June 2007! He did it faster than any other player before him.

Ryan reached 200 career home runs in July 2009! He did it faster than any other player before him.

27

Making Time for Fans

Ryan often makes time to talk to his fans.

Timeline

1979 Ryan is born in St. Louis, Missouri.

1994 Ryan begins playing high school baseball.

1998 Ryan begins playing for the Missouri State Bears.

2004 Ryan joins the Philadelphia Phillies.

2005 Ryan wins the Rookie of the Year award.

2006 Ryan wins an award for Most Valuable Player.

2008 Ryan helps the Phillies win the World Series.

2009 Ryan reaches 200 career home runs.

For More Information

Books:

Frisch, Aaron. *Philadelphia Phillies*. Mankato, MN: Creative Education, 2009.

Herzog, Brad. *H Is for Home Run: A Baseball Alphabet*. Chelsea, MI: Sleeping Bear Press, 2004.

Rasemas, Joe, and Patrice Sherman. *Ryan Howard*. Hockessin, DE: Mitchell Lane Publishers, 2009.

Savage, Jeff. *Ryan Howard*. Minneapolis, MN: Lerner Publications, 2008.

Web Sites:

Major League Baseball: Ryan Howard

www.mlb.com/team/player.jsp?player_id=429667

The Philadelphia Phillies: Ryan Howard

philadelphia.phillies.mlb.com/team/player_career.jsp?player_id=429667

Glossary

award: a prize given to someone for doing something well

career: in sports, the time a player is a pro

college: a school some people go to after high school

pro: someone who gets paid to play a sport

rookie: someone who is new to a job or sports league

valuable: thought highly of because of personal abilities

Index